Observations of
"Just a Housewife"

※

Beryl Billenness

Copyright © 2013 Beryl Billenness
All rights reserved.

ISBN: 1479319406
ISBN-13: 9781479319404

From Beryl Bellerness
who loved being with you all

Preface

I may be just a housewife, and it's not everyone's cup of tea,
But on behalf of all the others, do you mind if I make a plea.
To do the job efficiently, takes common sense and dedication,
And it's also brought, at least for me, a lot of satisfaction.

I dedicate this book to our two lovely daughters, Stevie for her determination in getting it published and also Lesley for all the help she has given me in so many other ways.

Also with special thanks to Steve my son-in-law for styling the front cover.

Beryl Billenness

For Better for Worse

The ups and downs of married life,
The tears the fears the conflicts the strife.

The feelings of contentment are sometimes quite rare,
You say to yourself was ever love there.

We get those feelings one time or another,
You even consider going home to your mother.

Then the troubles are over, the battles have been won,
And the look in his eye, tells you he's still the one.

You kiss and cuddle forgive and forget,
And look at the last weeks with a lot of regret.

So don't give up at the occasional hitch,
Remember at the best of times, life can still be a bitch.

Gone but not Forgotten.

Why do my efforts end up a failure,
Why do they always finish up in Australia.

I put my plants in with such loving care,
A few month's later nothing's there.

Could it be insects or just lack of manure,
What ever it is, of one thing I'm sure.

If you go down under no doubt you will see,
A beautiful garden that belongs to me.
.

So Much for Youth

I'm beginning to enjoy life now I'm getting older,
Once I wouldn't say boo to a goose, but now I'm getting bolder.

I couldn't express an opinion, because my face went red,
Now with age and maturity, I can laugh at what's been said.

All ages have their bonuses, this one's the best for me,
At the ripe old age of sixty-one, I'm in my prime you see.

A Spoonful of Sugar

It seems to me since way way back,
I've been a bit of a hypochondriac.

Every day it's something new,
But it's nothing as simple as three day flu.

Whatever I've got it's serious I'm sure,
Still even the doctor's can't find a cure.

For the times I've said this must be the end,
It's enough to drive you round the bend.

I've had something wrong with most parts of me now,
Yet I've survived so far, and only God knows how.

And although I know what a misery I've been,
I'd like to get a telegram from the Queen.

You're Never too Old

I've made so many mistakes in my life,
I'd like to go back and put them right.

One can't see till it's far too late.
Could we have done different, or was it just fate.

We come into this world with no experience at all,
We do stupid things that make fools of us all.

It's nice to know that as we get older,
Most of us also get a bit wiser.

Don't Give Up

Not exactly Einstein is what my husband said,
Strong in the arm, but a little bit weak in the head.

Surrounded by so much intelligence, I thought he must be right,
The family's all computer mad, why can't I be as bright.

The minute I'm asked a question, it's then I always find,
When brains were being handed out, that I was way behind.

But recently there's been a change, something's come to light,
I'm not such a dunderhead after all, I have the gift to write.

So don't let these stupid thoughts drive you to despair,
There's always something for which you have a flair.

You're a Long Time Dead

Do you ever wonder, what we're doing in this world?
Would you like to see the mysteries of your life unfurled?

Where are we going, what is our aim?
There's one thing for certain, life isn't a game.

Most of us don't know what it's all about,
That it's getting more complicated, there is no doubt.

Work! Work! Work! there's such a lot to be done,
Surely we realise there should also be fun.

We need such a lot to keep up with the Jones's,
We won't relax, till we're a heap of bones.

What's it all for, is this how we're supposed to behave?
To work ourselves into an early grave.

Just take it easy and with your partner,
Plan for more leisure, more loving, more laughter.

It's a wonderful world enjoy it, don't sit and moan,
The decision in the end is your very own.

Who am I

For so many years I have been someone else,
Now it is time to be myself.

But who is the real me, can I make a new start,
For so long now I've been acting a part.

The part of a mother the part of a wife,
But I'm going to be me for the rest of my life.

I admire the sophisticates but that's not for me,
This is the one I'd choose to be.

The scruffily dressed me who potters all day,
And spends her time planning her next holiday.

Who dresses up occasionally when friends come for tea,
That's definitely the part that was made for me.

A Dream for the Future

Who is this strange old lady, running round in a pony and trap,
She's said to be eccentric, and often caught having a nap.

She wears her hair in an enormous bun, and her clothes are rather shabby,
She must be at least ninety years old, but doesn't act old or crabby.

She likes gardening and cooking, and invites neighbours in for tea,
The happiest times for her she says, is when writing her poetry.

She comes into the village and chats to one and all,
She's always willing to do her bit, if we need help at the village hall,

She has chickens in her garden and calls each one by name,
She likes all kinds of wildlife and some become quite tame.

She's quite a travelled lady, with many a tale to tell,
She talks on many subjects, but is an avid listener as well.

Who is this strange old lady, it's very clear to see
You guessed of course it's me.

Who Wants Reality

I'm just a day dreamer, I could sit and dream all day
It doesn't seem to bother me, that I dream my life away.

I've tried to stay in this world, with its trouble and its strife,
But in my little dream world, it's a much more peaceful life.

I have all sorts of day dreams, travelling far and wide,
Nothing is impossible, there're so many things I haven't tried.

I've had quite a lot of experiences, in reality
But it doesn't stop me dreaming, of things that are yet to be.

Going for Gold

My husband's such a hoarder, he won't throw things away,
Doesn't matter what it is, he'll make use of it one day.

Our loft is full of junk, because everything has its price,
I suppose I should be grateful, it's his one and only vice.

It's because I'm just the opposite, I find it so frustrating,
To see a load of junk just sitting there, and outside the dustbin's waiting.

But it would only make him angry, and I'd burst into tears,
I suppose I'd best leave well alone, for just a few more years.

I'd regret how I feel, of this I'm quite sure,
If he and his junk were not here any more.

A Bad Example

If there's one piece of advice I'd give to the young,
It's, don't do the things that I have done.

I've neglected my body I've neglected my mind,
But it's only now I'm beginning to find.

With a little more thought and a little more care,
I wouldn't be showing so much wear and tear.

My body is sagging it's no longer trim,
If I'd watched what I'd ate, I'd still be quite slim.

My teeth are now quite beyond repair,
If I'd visited the dentist, they'd still be all there.

Let's have more chocolate let's have more cake,
We don't see the results till it's far too late.

So don't do what I've done do as I say,
A little care each day is a small price to pay.

Killing Time

There must be more to life than this,
One can have too much leisure and bliss

For example this is what I'll probably be doing today,
To top it all rain is said to be on its way.

I've washed and breakfasted and been to the loo,
I've dressed and done the chores, as I usually do.

I'll just check that the house is all spic and span,
Before I flush myself away down the pan.

I check our bedrooms, no nothing's out of place,
Flick round with the duster, just in case.

Stevie's room yes that's OK,
If only someone would come and stay.

Toilet and shower rooms all clean and neat,
Now I have to find something to eat.

There's three more hours yet to kill,
Before Ken comes in to take his fill.

Continued:

Then it's on with the washing up, clear up yet again,
Now I'd like to go out, but it's pouring with rain.

Oh woe is me, what can I do,
I think I'll take a book and have a read in the loo.

But I can't sit here for the entire afternoon,
Instead of March I wish it was June.

Another three hours before it's time for tea,
At least then I'll have some company.

Now it's a question of what's for tea,
Kippers or eggs what will it be?

The last of the washing up's done for the day,
All tidy and everything put away.

It's telly then untill cocoa at ten,
Can't we do something different now and then.

I have what's known as wedded bliss, even so,
There must be more to life than this, you know.

What Price Fame

You can't take it with you, so it is said,
Then why is it painters don't find fame till their dead.

Where does the money go, please put me wise,
Do the talented come back in another guise.

To collect their earnings which have accrued,
For painting a model, year's ago in the nude.

It's a mystery for sure we'll never know,
But just in case it's worth having a go.

What Price Relations

They say I should be sorry, I should apologise to one and all,
I should have done it properly, and hired a great big hall.

I didn't have to prepare the food, or make a wedding cake,
I did it all completely wrong, and there's lessons I ought to take.

What we did for the wedding day, was an absolute disgrace,
Relatives come first you know, bride and groom take second place.

I'm a mother of three and I'm sixty four,
But I feel I can't think for myself any more.

With instructions coming in even over the phone,
Any more of this and I'll soon leave home.

So we'll have another wedding day, and choose a nice big room,
We'll have food and drinks and relatives, and to hell with the bride and groom.

Ode to my Garden

Sitting in my garden room, my husband made for me,
I'm so grateful for the sight I have, which enables me to see.

So many lovely shrubs and flowers, of different scent and hue,
I could sit here so contented, just drinking in the view.

Birds playing in the bird bath are such a delight to see,
We even have a hedgehog, which comes in for a midnight feed.

I've grown to love this garden, just as the lady did before,
I've carried on with her labour of love, and each day love it more.

The garden's been on loan to us, we've done the best we could.
To make it look loved and cherished, as we think all gardens should.

Au Revoir

We asked our niece Susan to pay us a call,
To watch a video of us all.

It was whilst she was here we became aware,
That a strong smell of garlic filled the air.

Two cloves of garlic she ate every day,
The benefit's of which she felt straightaway.

We love our niece Susan but because of the pong,
We were all very pleased she didn't stay too long.

Overboard

I'm sure this sailing lark's not for me,
In more ways than one, I feel all at sea.

There's such a lot I have to learn,
But I do know the difference between the bow and the stern.

I have to bend double to clean the loo,
And cooking in the galley is a problem too.

Navigation is a thing I'll never learn to do,
How do we get there I haven't a clue.

There's warps and fenders and halyards and such,
These names I get muddled, they confuse me so much.

There's cleats and sheets and a thing called a winch,
If I could remember all these, it would be a cinch.

I'm covered in bruises, I'm all black and blue,
My nose is also quite colourful too.

But I have to keep at it the "Captain" said,
So I'll just take my book, and have a read in "the head"

Who's a Pretty Boy Then

Just think of a baby so cuddly and cute,
Skin like peaches and cream, he's a regular beaut.

Dimples on cheeks, knees and elbows he's got,
He chuckles when you tickle him, he's loved such a lot.

And when he does something naughty, you say never mind,
But just change his nappy and clean his chubby behind.

Think of an old man sitting in his chair,
Teeth in a glass, and very little hair.

His clothes are rather shabby, he's got dribbles down his front,
And no one seems to care for him, cos all he does is grunt.

Same human being, same name, same heart,
Just many years apart.

Summer

It's so quiet sitting peacefully on the beach,
Blue skies, warm sun, and a calm sea at my feet.

Not a word needs to be said,
Just the sounds of the sea-gulls flying overhead.

To be alone but not lonely, is Gods gift to me,
But how can you be lonely, sitting quietly by the sea.

Autumn Days

Deserted sea-front, no one else in sight,
Better than when the season's at its height.

Autumn sunshine, a light breeze is blowing,
Mind and bodies at peace, the sense of happiness is growing.

Back to chores and reality, the thought fills me with sorrow,
Still never mind, there's always tomorrow.

Sisters

It's lovely having you as my big sister,
Although you've always called me your skin and blister.

We don't see each other as much as we should,
I'd like to see more of you if only we could.

I remember the times we've had in the past,
Our eyes would just meet, and we'd do nothing but laugh.

We'd giggle and giggle till our eyes filled with tears,
May those times recur for many more years.

And as the years we've been Sisters slowly increase,
May our love for each other never decrease

Just too Busy

I'd love to make fresh scones for tea,
If I could only be sure of some company.

A lovely fruit cake, or some nice jam tarts,
But with my family so busy, I begin to lose heart.

It seems life is going at such a pace,
What's going to become of the human race.

Everyone's rushing here and there,
There is no time to stand and stare.

You'd think with all the labour saving machines,
They'd have more time for the simple things.

They haven't the time, there's too much to be done,
But I'll still make my scones, blow it just for one.

A Thought for today

I want to die on a summer's day, when the sun is at its height,
Not on a cold and frosty day, though the snow is shining white.

I want to die on a happy day when my heart is fit to burst,
Not on a day when I'm feeling so ill, and the pain is at its worst.

If we had one wish we'd all wish the same,
To die with dignity, and not in great pain.

Dreaming

I'd love to live on an island, one of my own choice,
It would have a tiny house on it, with a few mod cons of course.

No fertilizers or pollutants, they're not for me,
Everything as God intended, all grown naturally.

None of the noise we live with today,
Just the sound of the sea flowing gently in the bay.

I'd listen to the birds, and the wind whispering thru the trees,
I'd run barefoot thru the grass, and do just as I please.

I'd probably be bored at the end of the month,
But I'd still like to try it just the once.

Regression

I'd love to go back in history,
To see life as it used to be.

A time in each century I'd ask for that's all,
Just give me a chance to be a fly on the wall.

Eeny Meeny Miny Mo

We've all heard of the mystical Tom Dick and Harry,
There's a similar lot here now, but called Neil, John and Paddy.

Which one do we vote for, which one is the best,
He'll have to be good to get us out of this mess.

With a face full of smiles, they walk around,
The promises they make, how genuine they sound.

They argue and boast like kids do in school,
They take us all for right stupid fools.

We know its all talk, and not much will be done,
But my vote is for Paddy, the good looking one.

Back to Basics

It's a pity kids think vandalisms such fun,
It costs the tax-payer a tidy sum.

Every day there's results of something they've done,
Will the war between us ever be won.

The excuse it's unemployment poor housing and such,
Is a load of rubbish and doesn't convince me much.

It's our generation that should take part of the blame,
We're teaching them the wrong things again and again.

Most of the young are doing just fine,
It's a small minority that should toe the line.

More discipline is what's needed in the world today,
If it's not going to fall into the depths of decay.

Money isn't Everything

Lakes, Rivers, Forests and Meadows, treasures of such beauty,
but what's happening to our land,
Man is destroying it, with gigantic sweeps of his oh so greedy hand.

Don't lets think of tomorrow, sharing such beauty with future generations,
Let's get all we can to-day, like every other nation.

I despair of man and his high aspirations,
That his very intelligence, could mean the end of civilisation.

Using that intelligence for the good, it's great,
But it's making us far too greedy, we must stop before it's too late.

Let's turn back the clock, don't consider wealth,
Think of the most important thing of all, and that's our future health.

16 January 1991

The war on Kuwait has started today,
We hope God willing it's not here to stay.

The fodder with which the guns are being fed,
Could be filling the mouths, of the third world instead.

So much money spent on destruction,
Why can't it be used instead, for creation.

I believe in God but I wish he'd explain,
Why men exist, such as Hussein.

Stop Lights

Why do the traffic lights lay our characters so bare,
A woman looks in the mirror and tidies her hair.

Whilst the male species, as everyone knows,
Just sits there quietly picking his nose.

So Much for TV

TV brings so much pleasure to the young and to the old,
To the ordinary family, it's worth its weight in gold.

Compared to other countries, I think the programmes here are fine,
It's when sex and violence rear there heads, I wish they'd draw the line.

They say parents are responsible for what their children view,
Can't they see that's an impossible thing to do.

The video's in shops around, are going from bad to worse,
Whatever the context they're not concerned, its money in the purse.

It's in context, it was done in good taste, that's the usual patter,
But as long as money keeps rolling in, what we think doesn't matter.

Continued:

TV doesn't influence people, just listen to their gall,
They might convince themselves of this, they don't convince me at all

TV can teach us many things, we know it's here to stay,
But let's have reflections of what life should be, and not what it is today.

How Time Flies

We come into this world with no teeth and very little hair,
Our skin is all wrinkled and we need constant care.

At the age of ten we have spots galore,
Glasses and freckles that we abhore.

At twenty our bums are too big, and our boobs are too small,
But our legs are real nice, and who's perfect after all.

At thirty years old we feel quite mature,
We're married now and no longer pure.

With three young children the work is no joke.
To make matters worse we're always broke.

At forty the change of life begins, the menopause,
Things start to happen, what could be the cause.

At fifty it's finished, one feels over the hill,
Your kids are not married but they're on the pill.

Continued:

You think when the kids leave home, that's the end of the pain,
But you pick up the pieces again and again.

Sixty's a time for a hobby or two,
But the kids need your help, they're in a frightful stew.

At seventy your children are settled, they're happy at last,
We begin to reminisce, to remember the past.

It's a sure sign of old age when you start doing that,
We must sell the house and buy a flat.

At eighty we think it's time to relax,
No more worries about income tax.

Still there are many other worries in store,
Like rheumatism, bunions and I can't hear much anymore.

It seems such a short time since we were young,
But with wrinkles, no hair and toothless gums, we're surely back to where we begun.

More Please

Healthy eating is just not my scene,
Will it really make me healthy and lean.

Fresh fruit, and veggies, salads and such,
Are not terribly interesting, I don't like them very much.

Whereas suety puddings, and lovely plum duff,
Anything fattening is my kind of stuff.

Despite eating all the wrong kinds of food,
I'm just well rounded and feel really good.

Early Viewing Recommended

Gingerly opening the front door there,
Yes, it's definitely in need of some tender loving care.

Grubby windows, bare boards, some which are creaking,
Such a lot to be done, my spirit is weakening.

Everything looks so shabby and neglected,
Yes, it's just as we suspected.

Fully furnished it looked so nice,
But empty as it is now, we'd not have looked at it twice.

The wall's which I thought were OK before,
Are faded where pictures have hung, and there's hole's galore.

The garden too is in a frightful mess,
Is it true that hard work is good for stress.

If so I guarantee that in three months time,
We'll both have collapsed or be in our prime.

Growing Old Disgracefully

It's nice to be eccentric, friends never know what to expect,
Whatever you do, and whatever you've done, you never seem to lose their respect

It's a word that allows you to do what you like,
In the dead of winter, you can go fly your kite.

You can be as rude as you like, slam your door in their face,
But they'll still find you amusing, and think" what a case".

It's a word you'll hear often whilst having a go,
"You'll have to excuse her, she's eccentric you know"

Why Me

It's was nice having five big brothers, with me the only girl,
And although I was christened Beryl, my mum always called me Berl

She much preferred boys she said, I never understood why,
I can always remember her saying it, from about the age of five.

Why did she say it? Now I'll never know,
Perhaps that would explain why, my self-esteem is rather low.

Out of three girls born alive,
Why was I the only one, chosen to survive.

Still I've had a happy life, despite the ups and downs,
And expressing myself in poetry, I can really go to town.

But I really loved my mum, and when all's said and done,
That's a good enough reason, to have been the chosen one.

Time for a Change

What a lovely world we live in today,
What the hell does it matter if you're lesbian or gay.

Drugs and drinks they all abound,
There's one parent families all around.

There's muggings and road-rage, whatever next.
Old ladies getting raped, there's just no respect.

There's too many do-gooders, let the punishment fit the crime,
A few strokes of the birch, not just a fine.

Women's lib is a freedom most females sought,
But they finish up with a kid living on income support

Bring back hanging, the stocks and the birch,
An eye for an eye, hit them where it hurts.

There's additives in our food, hormones in our meat,
Can anyone tell me what is fit to eat.

Continued:

They tell you in one breath that's good for you,
The next minute they're telling you something new.

Watching the government work is like watching a farce,
If it wasn't so serious you'd have to laugh.

Skin Deep

My face never was my fortune, I think it's rather sad,
My hair was the one claim to beauty, that I ever had

Like ripe corn in a field, one young man said,
Now it's fading fast, and will soon be grey instead.

No it's my face and neck that are the trouble,
The wrinkles and lines seem to be coming at the double.

Where will it all end, I ask with a frown,
Everything seems to be hanging down.

If I make a success of this book you'll soon see,
With the money I make, there'll be a new me.

I suppose in the end we all go to pot,
But my sense of humour's still there, and that's worth a lot.

No longer True

My arms are empty, my lap is too.
I thought by now I'd have a grandchild or two.

We'd be great grand-parents, your dad and I,
But we've given up hope as the years go by.

We'd love to have taken them by the hand,
And gone on the beach, to play in the sand.

We'd make sand castles till the sun goes down,
Then buy them ice cream after a walk into town.

You'd come round with the kids for afternoon tea,
Or go and have a picnic by the sea.

There's such a lot of things we could have done,
Just being with them could have been such fun.

But I suppose in the end we shouldn't make a fuss,
Cos we've two lovely girls who are a joy to us

Still I hope they won't regret in years to come,
Being just a wife, and not a Mum.

The Simple Life for Me

Let me go back to a simple life, life as it used to be,
It all seems such a worry, and too complicated for the likes of me.

When cash was the only way to pay,
With a little put by for a rainy day.

No rubbish coming in every day with the post,
That's one of the things I hate the most.

Along with the packaging that I can't undo,
And the bottles I can't open, they're a problem too.

Getting through to the Bank or the Doc's on the phone,
Gets me so agitated I do nothing but moan.

There're so many things I would miss no doubt,
But a whole lot more I could do without.

Such Good Times

We never know what life has in store,
We don't appreciate what we've got till it's not there anymore.

All those good times we've had in the past,
I suppose, were just too good to ever last.

I loved dropping in for a nice cup of tea.
After having a stroll on the front by the sea.

Sometimes on a Sunday we'd decide what to do,
Perhaps at the boot-fare we'd find a bargain or two.

Or go and watch Abi at her riding school,
You could tell at a glance she was having a ball.

Then we'd come back home and have a nice meal,
I'm missing all that I can't help how I feel.

But I must stop feeling, so sorry for myself,
And be grateful you're all happy, and in good health.

There's Still Time

I'm getting old and the end is nigh,
But the time I have left is passing me by.

There's so many things I still want to do,
And I want to do something completely new.

I want to cross Australia on that really slow train,
Or buy a boat and moor it in Spain.

See all the places that are there to see,
But whatever happens, it's all down to me.

So I'll have to be grateful for what we've already done,
And grateful that it was all such fun.

Dementia

Where is my husband? where has he gone?
This isn't the man I've loved for so long.

I've loved and respected him for so many years,
But to see him now, makes my eyes fill with tears.

He's been such a good husband, and such a good dad,
And dealt so well with the few problems we've had.

When I think of the holidays, and the good times we've had,
They're all in the past, it's really quite sad.

But he seems so contented in our nice little flat,
And unaware of what's happening, I'm grateful for that

So the cuddles I sometimes get are worth such a lot,
Cos we have to make the best, of the time we've still got.

A Father's Love

Whatever the troubles I may have had,
I've always known I could rely on my dad.

You're quiet unassuming and don't like being praised,
But knowing you're there, what a difference it's made.

You're so pleased to see me whatever time of day,
And you're always there, at the end of the day.

You're someone I look up to, someone I respect,
You're a dad in a million, you're one of the best.

Whatever's in the future, be it laughter or tears,
May we be there for each other, for many more years.

For My Niece

We rely on our Mums to always be there,
To love and cherish us and show that they care.

We never forget them cos they're no longer here,
But think of them as someone, we held very dear.

When you think of your Mum now, your eyes fill with tears,
But it will get easier in the oncoming years.

This Modern World

I'm the head of a gang, but only eleven years old,
The kids know whose boss, and do as they're told.

We don't go to school much anymore,
We have a lot more fun at the local store.

We nick sweets and drinks and just help ourselves,
Then we empty the cans, and put them back on the shelves.

Because of our age there's nothing they can do,
That applies to the cops and our parents too.

My parents are not bothered, they're out to work every day,
I make myself scarce, and keep out their of way.

We rough the old men up when they're on their own,
Whilst I take a few shots on my mobile phone.

As for the old dears, well, we just pinch their bags,
And use the cash that's in 'em to keep us in fags.

My conscience is clear cos we're just having fun,
I don't look to the future, cos I'm gonna die young.

* * *

Continued:

I can't believe it, yes I'm eighty one,
I was so sure I'd die when I was still quite young.

I have so many regrets for what I did,
I thought I knew it all when I was a kid.

I'm getting my come- uppance you can be sure of that,
Cos my missus and I were quite happy in our one bedroom flat,

Till she got mugged and knocked down, it only happened last week,
She'd been to get our pensions, cos I've trouble with me feet.

She died from the shock, now I'm all alone,
I don't like going out, I feel nervous on me own.

I know the regrets that I have won't go away,
They'll be there forever till my dying day.

Such a Pity

I don't envy them much, the kids of today,
When you think of the temptations that are there for them,
every day.

The drinks and drugs the violence on TV
The damage it's doing for us all to see,

If they pick up the rubbish that's shown on TV,
It's no wonder they've no respect, for you or for me.

They say they get bored, once they come home from school,
So they get into mischief, and start acting the
fool.

With no one to correct them what is to be done,
Cos breaking the law, to them is just fun.

They have so much more than we ever had,
So why the discontent, it's really so sad.

To our Sons and Daughters

You know we love you, just as you love us,
But please understand, we don't like making a fuss.

It's nice to know you're always there,
If things, sometimes, get hard to bear.

But dignity to the elderly, is a very important thing,
And please believe us, we don't like to give in.

I know we wrinklies can be difficult at times,
But when we're past it, you'll soon see the signs.

Euthanasia

How much longer must I live with this terrible pain,
Cos my pleas for release are all in vain.

There are so many out there, who are just like me,
Who would welcome death, just to be pain free.

Let the ones who say we're playing God,
Finish up like me, a poor helpless sod.

My body's a mess, but nothings wrong with my head,
Why can't they believe I'd rather be dead.

The pills I've saved, are up on that shelf,
But I'm too bloody helpless, to take them myself.

For a long time now I've felt over the hill,
But now it's time for that long awaited pill.

Knowing my wish has been granted, and the pain will soon cease,
The nightmare has ended, and I'll soon be at peace.

In Memory of my Brother

We take family for granted, think they'll always be there,
Then suddenly they've gone, and we're left in despair,

Up until April, life for my brother was great,
In Janet his wife, he'd found a good mate.

They enjoyed life to the full no matter what they did,
He was so full of energy, just like a big kid

He liked friends coming round, for drinks and a snack,
And looked forward to be invited back.

He had such a loud voice, yes we used to complain,
But it saddens us now, to know we'll never hear it again.

I believe in God, but I wish he'd explain
Why such a good man, should suffer such pain

Thing's Aren't What They Used to Be

Think of a child fifty years ago,
The contentment we got, from watching them grow.

The simple things they did every day,
And the pleasure we got from watching them play.

We had no money for costly toys,
So there were dolls for girls, and train sets for boys.

With their buckets and spades, and a helping hand from me,
They'd play quite happily all day by the sea.

Let's pretend was all part of the game,
They used their imagination, they all did the same.

They loved playing shops, using make-believe money,
And the things they'd have for sale, were really quite funny.

They'd collect grasses and berries that grew wild all around,
And anything unusual they sometimes found.

Nothing was sold cos they were just having fun,
Being together with friends out in the sun

* * *

Are we Happier Now

What a difference it is in the World today,
No time for childhood no time for play.

So much pressure to do well at school,
But if you have common sense, you'll not be considered a fool.

With most of the work done on computers and such,
Man power won't come into it very much.

From the age of five kids will be taught about sex,
And about being gay, what will it be next.

We're making them grow up, but it's much to fast,
Let them enjoy life, and be carefree, whilst it lasts.

We mustn't make a point of whether they're girls or boys,
So it's train sets for girls and dolls for boys.

They spend time indoors instead of out in the sun,
But playing with electronics they think, is just great fun.

What's in the future? It's just as well we can't tell,
It's all down to us be it heaven or hell.

About the Author

Having had five brothers who are sadly no longer here, I have grown up to be quite a tom-boy in my actions, and thinking. I had to have quite a thick skin too and a good sense of humour, which is not a bad thing. We have two lovely caring daughters. We couldn't wish for better. Our son, who we shall never forget, committed suicide at the age of 29yrs. But we all have our crosses to bear, and now my lovely husband, who has been my hero for 60 yrs, has been diagnosed with dementia but is in no pain and seems quite happy with my care. I find writing my poems helps me to express my inner most feelings. Some poems have been asked for by friends and relatives and I do my best writing them. May it give you some pleasure in reading them.

Made in the USA
Columbia, SC
30 October 2017